Wilson Reading System®

Student Workbook
Three B

THIRD EDITION

by Barbara A. Wilson

Wilson Language Training Corporation

www.wilsonlanguage.com

Wilson Reading System® Student Workbook Three B

Item # SW3B

ISBN 978-1-56778-096-3

THIRD EDITION (revised 2004)

The Wilson Reading System is published by:

Wilson Language Training Corporation
47 Old Webster Road
Oxford, MA 01540
United States of America

(800) 899-8454

www.wilsonlanguage.com

Printed in the U.S.A.

May 2006

Read the first syllable with the second syllable. Cover the divided word and write the word on the line. Uncover the divided word and check spelling. Read the written words.

ban - dit   = _____   meth - od   = _____

dis - miss   = _____   sock - et   = _____

pop - lin   = _____   pel - let   = _____

pep - sin   = _____   gal - lop   = _____

As - pen   = _____   an - them   = _____

mag - net   = _____   can - vas   = _____

rus - tic   = _____   san - dal   = _____

rap - id   = _____   tin - sel   = _____

van - ish   = _____   nov - el   = _____

gam - ut   = _____   sig - nal   = _____

Combine the first syllable with the second syllable to read the word. Cover the divided word and write the word on the line. Uncover the divided word and check spelling. Read the written words.

whip - lash = _____   cat - nap = _____

sum - mit = _____   sun - bath = _____

pic - nic = _____   pot - shot = _____

pub - lic = _____   hub - cap = _____

gos - sip = _____   Wil - lis = _____

com - bat = _____   lim - pid = _____

pun - ish = _____   rap - id = _____

hel - met = _____   hec - tic = _____

rel - ish = _____   wit - ness = _____

nut - shell = _____   cal - lus = _____

Read the sentence. Select the correct word from the box to complete the sentence. Write the word on the line. Reread the completed sentence. Use each word in the box only once.

picnic	habit	exam	toxic	jacket
sunfish	profit	cabin	whiplash	cactus

1 Did Sanchez go to the class _____?

2 Tom got a _____ with his rod.

3 Did Fran get _____ in the crash?

4 That _____ plant must get some sun.

5 I think the _____ is a mess.

6 I hid the cash _____ in the desk.

7 I felt sick from the _____ gas.

8 Will we have a math _____?

9 Stan left the ticket in his _____ pocket.

10 Bill has a bad _____.

The Day Trip

_____They sat in the hot sun.

_____Babs and Ed went to a rustic cabin on the summit of a hill.

_____A cold wind hit them.

_____Then they had lunch in the cabin.

_____Babs and Ed *saw* the vivid sunset.

Write the sentences above in the correct order on the lines below.

1 _____

2 _____

3 _____

4 _____

5 _____

Read the syllables on each side of the box. Draw a line to connect syllables to form real words.

sub	bat
com	pus
cam	mit

rus	tic
tim	id
kid	nap

rock	lic
pub	et
ad	mit

pub	vet
eth	nic
vel	lish

cred	ic
pan	it
self	ish

ban	ish
frol	rich
en	ic

Write the words above on the lines below.

_____   _____   _____

_____   _____   _____

_____   _____   _____

_____   _____   _____

_____   _____   _____

Read the syllables on each side of the box. Draw a line to connect syllables to form real words.

mus	ish
rad	tang
gal	lop

hel	gun
shot	cum
tal	met

den	it
ed	id
viv	im

ex	in
cab	ish
van	pel

pol	dit
gob	len
ban	lin

tick	am
ex	et
sol	id

Write the words above on the lines below.

_____   _____   _____

_____   _____   _____

_____   _____   _____

_____   _____   _____

_____   _____   _____

Divide each word below into syllables. Read the word. Write the syllables on the lines.

catnip   = _____ _____   chitchat = _____ _____

victim   = _____ _____   humbug   = _____ _____

valid   = _____ _____   expel   = _____ _____

rapid   = _____ _____   ringlet = _____ _____

tactic   = _____ _____   menthol = _____ _____

vanish   = _____ _____   limit   = _____ _____

mustang = _____ _____   muffin   = _____ _____

model   = _____ _____   zigzag   = _____ _____

gossip   = _____ _____   velvet   = _____ _____

rustic   = _____ _____   tennis   = _____ _____

pocket   = _____ _____   cosmic   = _____ _____

profit   = _____ _____   mimic   = _____ _____

timid   = _____ _____   campus   = _____ _____

tonic   = _____ _____   credit   = _____ _____

admit   = _____ _____   ticket   = _____ _____

Underline or "scoop" the two syllables. Mark the syllables with a **c** to indicate a closed syllable. Put a breve (˘) above the short vowels. Read the words.

EXAMPLE: <u>sŭn</u> <u>fĭsh</u>
    c   c

sunfish	banquet	vanish	victim
magnet	goblin	mascot	sonnet
nutshell	jonquil	upset	sudden
expel	misfit	bonnet	cobweb
callus	bedbug	shellfish	topic
shut-off	humbug	impel	gunman
Dublin	quintet	bandit	enrich
habit	freshen	candid	hobnob
summit	campus	pipkin	sublet
chitchat	mantis	kidnap	septic
annex	witness	rustic	dismiss

Underline or "scoop" the two syllables. Mark the syllables with a **c** to indicate a closed syllable. Put a breve (˘) above the short vowels. Read the nonsense words.

EXAMPLE: <u>gŏs</u> <u>pĕn</u>
     c   c

gospen	galnic	helpon	aspit
debish	conpun	kidtic	pinmus
rabcot	optil	napfin	popmeg
litship	pepmop	hapmon	besnet
velvin	casbit	ziglid	tenlin
tipdex	sonmic	findid	hobnum
bishbat	jonlen	paltin	fampel
enset	vicdon	shotlet	taltic
musfit	tencum	tuplet	azbim
tholpun	quislet	gussot	ibot
polit	famjan	pippet	nixib

Combine the first syllable with the second syllable to read the word. Cover the divided word and write the word on the line. Uncover the divided word and check spelling. Read the written words.

in - sult   = _____   plas - tic   = _____

ex - tent   = _____   sand - box   = _____

in - dent   = _____   tres - pass   = _____

snap - shot   = _____   com - plex   = _____

hun - dred   = _____   trans - mit   = _____

fish - pond   = _____   dras - tic   = _____

den - tist   = _____   milk - man   = _____

in - tend   = _____   bank - rupt   = _____

hand - cuff   = _____   at - tempt   = _____

drop - cloth   = _____   ad - dress   = _____

im - pend   = _____   mod - est   = _____

en - chant   = _____   tran - quil   = _____

ten - dril   = _____   gas - tric   = _____

con - trast   = _____   min - strel   = _____

em - blem   = _____   en - trap   = _____

Read the syllables on each side of the box. Draw a line to connect syllables to form real words.

trans	mand
com	tress
ac	plant

an	tic
rad	press
im	isht

lip	band
seg	ment
hus	stick

hold	sist
im	plant
in	up

ex	fin
cof	press
in	fest

cul	plex
com	prit
ex	tend

Write the words above on the lines below.

_____   _____   _____

_____   _____   _____

_____   _____   _____

_____   _____   _____

_____   _____   _____

Read the sentence. Select the correct word from the box to complete the sentence. Write the word on the line. Use each word in the box only once. Copy the completed sentence on the lines provided. Add capital letters and punctuation.

landfill	trespass	clinic	impress	insist

1 the pup must go to the vet at the pet_____

_____

_____

2 this _____will not hold much trash

_____

_____

3 we cannot _____ in that sandlot

_____

_____

4 mom will _____ that I got this cold from the draft in the den

_____

_____

5 sam will _____ his gal with that ring

_____

_____

Select a syllable from the top of each box to form real words. Write the syllable on the line. Read the word.

mat span den
_____dex
_____tress
_____tist

com ab in
_____land
_____plex
_____sent

pend vent lift
de_____
up_____
in_____

en con up
_____hold
_____tent
_____gulf

tic mit et
plan_____
fran_____
trans_____

rel ex seg
_____ish
_____ment
_____tent

dent ish tic
plas_____
blem_____
in_____

bag tic ic
hand_____
clin_____
spas_____

cul ex in
_____empt
_____ept
_____prit

Divide each word below into syllables. Read the word. Write the syllables on the lines.

extent = _____ _____   shipment = _____ _____

insult = _____ _____   tranquil = _____ _____

disgust = _____ _____   insist = _____ _____

expand = _____ _____   offend = _____ _____

skillet = _____ _____   skeptic = _____ _____

clinic = _____ _____   drastic = _____ _____

intend = _____ _____   figment = _____ _____

plastic = _____ _____   dragnet = _____ _____

infest = _____ _____   attend = _____ _____

sunlamp = _____ _____   disrupt = _____ _____

sandwich = _____ _____   traffic = _____ _____

children = _____ _____   address = _____ _____

nonstop = _____ _____   splendid = _____ _____

Alfred = _____ _____   seventh = _____ _____

hamstring = _____ _____   empress = _____ _____

Divide each word below into syllables. Read the word. Write the syllables on the lines.

inscript = ____ ____

express = ____ ____

fishpond = ____ ____

entrap = ____ ____

slingshot = ____ ____

handbag = ____ ____

wildcat = ____ ____

pigskin = ____ ____

culprit = ____ ____

enrich = ____ ____

convent = ____ ____

pretzel = ____ ____

flannel = ____ ____

problem = ____ ____

handstand = ____ ____

gumdrop = ____ ____

wingspan = ____ ____

bobsled = ____ ____

sandblast = ____ ____

snapshot = ____ ____

pumpkin = ____ ____

humdrum = ____ ____

stronghold = ____ ____

enchant = ____ ____

trellis = ____ ____

absent = ____ ____

kingdom = ____ ____

dragon = ____ ____

Find the 2-syllable words. Underline or "scoop" the two syllables. Mark the syllables with a **c** to indicate a closed syllable.
Put a breve (˘) to mark the short vowels. Read the words.

EXAMPLE: <u>cŏn</u> <u>tĕst</u>
       c   c

1   I intend to shop *for* a handbag.

2   Dennis had a lung transplant.

3   Ben will attempt to get the ax from his strongbox.

4   I will publish this when I finish the subplot.

5   The contest will be held on the west campus.

Write all the multisyllabic words on the lines below

---

1 _____ _____

2 _____ _____

3 _____ _____

4 _____ _____ _____

5 _____ _____

Underline or "scoop" the two syllables. Mark the syllables with a **c** to indicate a closed syllable. Put a breve (˘) above the short vowels. Read the nonsense words.

EXAMPLE: **wĭg glĕt**
       c   c

wigglet	flonnich	triddop
shupnest	shiblent	chinfrob
drennist	frentlap	troppit
plabbid	thibselt	fleppen
trendid	plimmut	trilmest
flidden	drappog	enflont
clupnet	thipnest	instom
podjift	timplet	contimp
stroplim	greffib	extrib
glisset	vambith	admest

Read the sentence. Select the correct word from the box to complete the sentence. Write the word on the line. Reread the completed sentence. Use each word in the box only once.

tantrum	suntan	intend	insist	pretzels

1 I _____ to shop *for* lunch.

2 His _____ is from a sunlamp.

3 The tot had a bad _____ with his dad.

4 Did Dad _____ that Ben take a nap?

5 The tonic and _____ are on the top shelf.

Rewrite the sentences on the lines below.

1 _____

_____

2 _____

_____

3 _____

_____

4 _____

_____

5 _____

_____

1   I expect a conflict on this job.

2   This will have a distinct impact on me.

3   We must inspect the land prospect.

4   I suspect that Mr. Smith will win in this district.

5   Meg will contact Frank to discuss the contract.

Write the words containing the **ct** blend on the lines below.

1   _____   _____

2   _____   _____

3   _____   _____

4   _____   _____

5   _____   _____

Combine the first syllable with the second syllable to read the word. Cover the divided word and write the word on the line. Uncover the divided word and check spelling. Read the written words.

com - pact = _____   con - flict = _____

con - vict = _____   con - coct = _____

con - tact = _____   dis - trict = _____

con - nect = _____   im - pact = _____

col - lect = _____   in - duct = _____

ex - pect = _____   sus - pect = _____

pros - pect = _____   in - flict = _____

ob - struct = _____   ex - tract = _____

ad - dict = _____   dis - tract = _____

ob - ject = _____   in - spect = _____

Read the story "Mr. Dunlop Helps" in Student Reader Three (page 61). Read each sentence below. Write **T** on the line if it is true and **F** if it is false. Use the student reader to check your answers.

Mr. Dunlop Helps

1 *Mr.* Dunlop's checks *were* in a big mess. ____

2 *Mrs.* Dunlop did not subtract the cash she spent. ____

3 *Mr.* Dunlop did not help his mom. ____

4 *Mrs.* Dunlop did not neglect her checks. ____

5 *Mrs.* Dunlop did not intend to let it happen ____ *again*.

Write the sentences above on the lines provided. Change the false sentences to true in order to accurately rewrite the story.

1 _____

_____

2 _____

_____

3 _____

_____

4 _____

_____

5 _____

_____

Underline or "scoop" the two syllables. Mark the syllables with a **c** to indicate a closed syllable. Put a breve (˘) above the short vowels. Read the words.

EXAMPLE: <u>cŏn</u> <u>dŭct</u>
     c   c

conduct	subject	object
compact	suspect	connect
inspect	exact	contract
instinct	abstract	addict
distinct	neglect	convict
collect	insect	affect
concoct	contact	conflict
prospect	distract	obstruct
expect	extract	impact
district	inflict	induct

Read the sentence. Select the correct word from the box to complete the sentence. Write the word on the line. Reread the completed sentence. Use each word in the box only once.

collect	convict	contact	expect	impact
conduct	distract	insects	subject	neglect

1 Did the van dent on _____?

2 We must _____ the project boss.

3 The _____ did not infest the trash can.

4 The cop had to handcuff the _____.

5 I did not _____ Beth to find a dress in that shop.

6 I think Kim has the best _____ in that class.

7 French is my best _____.

8 Do not _____ Tom when he is in class.

9 Ken must _____ his cash from the bank.

10 We cannot _____ to finish the script.

Write the syllable from the top of each box on the lines to form real words. Read the words.

pect	duct	fect
ex_____	ab_____	in_____
pros_____	in_____	af_____
sus_____	con_____	ef_____

tract	ject	tinct
ex_____	ob_____	ex_____
dis_____	sub_____	ins_____
con_____	in_____	dis_____

Write the words above on the lines below. Underline **ct** blends.

_____ _____ _____

_____ _____ _____

_____ _____ _____

_____ _____ _____

_____ _____ _____

Read the sentences. Underline or "scoop" the syllables in the 2-syllable words.

1 the insects bit kim on the leg and kept her on the bench

2 i suspect that we will get sun in the pressbox

3 the conflict with fred upset his mom

4 can we inspect the job within the contract

5 i did not think that mr. flint *would* neglect his job

Write each sentence on the lines provided below. Add capital letters and punctuation.

1 _____

_____

2 _____

_____

3 _____

_____

4 _____

_____

5 _____

_____

Nonsense Words

Cross out any nonsense syllable that is not closed. Find and underline all closed syllables. Mark them with **c** to indicate a closed syllable. Mark the short vowels with a breve (˘). Read closed (underlined) syllables.

EXAMPLE: <u>clŭp</u>
      c

tract	prine	chait
toip	flet	nect
ust	flict	blish
neg	ing	fle
shene	trat	shemp
prog	fect	trung
com	stoad	crobe
fleam	pless	pact
ish	ject	und
trict	ble	clend

Combine the syllables to form a real word. Cover the divided word and write the word on the line. Uncover the divided word and check the spelling. Read the written word.

Wis - con - sin = _____

At - lan - tic = _____

vol - can - ic = _____

inv - vest - ment = _____

fan - tas - tic = _____

ath - let - ic = _____

ac - com - plish = _____

rec - om - mend = _____

con - sul - tant = _____

bad - min - ton = _____

in - trin - sic = _____

in - sis - tent = _____

con - sen - sus = _____

dis - con - tent = _____

dis - cred - it = _____

in - hab - it = _____

ex - is - tent = _____

in - hib - it = _____

as - ton - ish = _____

quin - tup - let = _____

Divide each word below into syllables. Read the word. Write the syllables on the lines.

Wisconsin = ____ ____ ____   intrinsic = ____ ____ ____

Atlantic = ____ ____ ____   insistent = ____ ____ ____

volcanic = ____ ____ ____   consensus = ____ ____ ____

investment = ____ ____ ____   discontent = ____ ____ ____

fantastic = ____ ____ ____   discredit = ____ ____ ____

athletic = ____ ____ ____   inhabit = ____ ____ ____

accomplish = ____ ____ ____   existent = ____ ____ ____

recommend = ____ ____ ____   inhibit = ____ ____ ____

consultant = ____ ____ ____   astonish = ____ ____ ____

badminton = ____ ____ ____   quintuplet = ____ ____ ____

Select a syllable from the top of each box to form real words. Write the syllable on the line. Read the word.

vest om sul
in____ment
con____tant
rec____mend

met con ex
in____act
sub____tract
cos____ic

net hib tup
mag____ic
quin____let
in____it

let cred val
dis____it
ath____ic
in____id

com sis con
con____tent
ac____plish
dis____nect

in ton lan
as____ish
dis____fect
At____tic

Write the words above on the lines below. Read the words.

_____   _____   _____

_____   _____   _____

_____   _____   _____

_____   _____   _____

Read the sentence. Select the correct word from the box to complete the sentence. Write the word on the line. Reread the completed sentence. Use each word in the box only once.

disconnect	athletic	investment
invalid	fantastic	embankment
badminton	congressman	Manhattan

1 The kids got the _____ set *for* a gift.

2 If *you* _____ the plug, the TV will shut off.

3 The _____ will win in this district.

4 This is a bad cash _____.

5 Ben's _____ skill is the best in the class.

6 Ed's _____ grin helps him.

7 The tall _____ will obstruct the path.

8 A trip to _____ can be lots of fun.

9 Do not collect the _____ tickets.

The Tennis Contest

1 Sam Captis was a _____.

2 He sat in the _____ *for* the tennis contest.

3 Greg Smith was the topmost _____.

4 _____had the talent to win, and he did this with much athletic skill.

5 Sam did think it was a _____ contest.

Copy the sentences above on the lines below. Underline 3-letter blends with three separate lines.

1 _____

2 _____

3 _____

4 _____

5 _____

Underline or "scoop" the syllables. Mark the syllables with a **c** to indicate a closed syllable. Read the words.

athletic	congressman	God-given
subcontract	consistent	commandment
insistent	columnist	Wisconsin
fantastic	investment	Atlantic
consultant	discredit	snapdragon
appendix	disconnect	hobgoblin
establish	discontent	Manhattan
volcanic	accomplish	recommend
assistant	badminton	embankment
quintuplet	invalid	inhabit

Find the 3-syllable words. Underline or "scoop" the three syllables. In each sentence there is one word misspelled. It is underlined. Rewrite the sentence correctly, including capitalization and punctuation. Proofread carefully.

1   mom is <u>frantik</u> about the investment plans

_____

2   did the <u>dentis</u> establish himself yet

_____

3   glen went to the <u>athletik</u> contest

_____

4   mr. griffin must <u>git</u> his appendix *out*

_____

5   elvis did not <u>sinng</u> in wilmington

_____

6   ed had lots of stuffing on <u>thankgiving</u>

_____

7   justin and calvin <u>wint</u> to manhattan

_____

8   ellen is <u>discontet</u> with her job

_____

9   the basketball <u>contes</u> was fantastic

_____

10   sid can <u>disconnekt</u> the old TV

_____

Add the suffix to each baseword. Write the whole word on the line. Underline the baseword and circle the suffix.

rent - ed   = _____   squint - ed   = _____

rent - ing   = _____   squint - ing   = _____

hand - ed   = _____   hunt - ed   = _____

hand - ing   = _____   hunt - ing   = _____

dust - ed   = _____   extend - ed   = _____

dust - ing   = _____   extend - ing   = _____

invent - ed   = _____   implant - ed   = _____

invent - ing = _____   implant - ing = _____

expect - ed   = _____   conduct - ed   = _____

expect - ing = _____   conduct - ing = _____

distract - ed = _____   enlist - ed   = _____

distract - ing = _____   enlist - ing   = _____

Read the word. Cover it. Write the baseword and the suffix on the lines provided.

crashing = _____ - _____   rusted = _____ - _____

shifting = _____ - _____   inducted = _____ - _____

sprinted = _____ - _____   drafting = _____ - _____

establishing = _____ - _____   insulted = _____ - _____

intended = _____ - _____   expanding = _____ - _____

finishing = _____ - _____   punishing = _____ - _____

splashing = _____ - _____   blinded = _____ - _____

grunted = _____ - _____   standing = _____ - _____

folded = _____ - _____   shrinking = _____ - _____

disgusted = _____ - _____   dented = _____ - _____

blinking = _____ - _____   twisted = _____ - _____

consulted = _____ - _____   investing = _____ - _____

1   The kids are standing in the back of the class.

2   Jim dented the rented van when he went on the
fishing trip.

3   We are expecting the bids *for* the subcontract.

4   Rob will get the lung transplanted in Wisconsin.

Write the words with suffixes on the lines below.

1   _____

2   _____   _____   _____

3   _____

4   _____

Vocabulary Practice

Create sentences that include the vocabulary words below. Use a dictionary or electronic spell checker as needed. Underline or "scoop" each syllable in the vocabulary words below.

3.1	3.2	3.3	3.4	3.5
famish	static	convict	consistent	invented
candid	transplant	compact	investment	consulting
vanquish	credit	suspect	discredit	implanted
rapid	complex	concoct	invalid	distracting
timid	segment	impact	columnist	transplanted
rustic	blemish	instinct		
toxin	contrast	conflict		
banish	culprit	abstract		
victim	extend	conduct		
expel	drastic	distinct		

Story Starter

At the end of Step 3 create a story that includes many (at least 5) of the vocabulary words below. This story takes place in a park. Underline each vocabulary word used from the list below.

upset	talent	suntan	fantastic
zigzag	sandlot	campus	windswept
until	basketball	tendon	pigskin
public	handspring	insects	sprinting
district	grasping	pivot	Midwest